W9-DEU-066

Super Sweet Sticker Book

SIZZLE PRESS

An imprint of Bonnier Publishing USA

251 Park Avenue South, New York, NY 10010

Copyright © 2018 by Viacom International Inc.

Manufactured in China HUH 0118

First published in Great Britain by Centum Books

First U.S. Edition

3 5 7 9 10 8 6 4 2

ISBN 978-1-4998-0733-2

sizzlepressbooks.com
bonnierpublishingusa.com

JoJo Gallery

CUTE and CRAZY!

Complete this sweet and sassy JoJo gallery. Which picture is your favorite?

Sticker

Pick out your favorite outfit!

#peaceouthaterz

RESPECT the bow!

Which bow style is your favorite?

GIRLS NEVER QUIT!

Sticker

Sticker

Bows are EVERYTHING!

3

Dance-off!

Do you love to dance as much as JoJo? Well, it's time to create your own dance sequences. Use the shadow stickers to create dance move sequences in the boxes below.

Remember, your final move should be awesome!

Sequence 1

LIVE TO DANCE

Final move

Sequence 2

LOVE TO DANCE

Final move

BE YOUR OWN Star

Try out your moves in front of a mirror.

Dance crew

Who will join you in your performance?
Write their names here:

....

....

....

....

....

....

Tasty Treats

OMG! A page full of yummy doughnuts!
Color them all in and decorate them
with your stickers.

JoJo Siwa

FOLLOW YOUR DREAMS

Juicy Pairs

First find the stickers, and place them on this page. Then circle all the matching pairs of juice. Which juice doesn't have a friend?

JOJO'S JUICE

Bow-the-Difference

Look at the spot the difference puzzles on these pages. When you spot a difference, mark it with a bow sticker from the sticker sheets.

1. Easy
3 differences

2. Medium
5 differences

3.

Hard
10 differences

See answers on page 40

Be Your Own Star!

Keep drawing around and around the star to create a cool pattern and fill this page. Then color it in and decorate with stickers.

Puzzle Pics

Complete these super cute pics of JoJo using the stickers.
Place a bow sticker next to your favorite pic.

a.

From My Heart

Yours

b.

BOW
Bow

c.

d.

See answers on page 40

Word Art

Stick

DREAM

Copy

Trace

DREAM

Stick

SUPER

Copy

Trace

SUPER

16

Stick

Star

Copy

Trace

Star

Now design your own word art and use stickers to decorate around it.

17

Juice Explosion!

JoJo pours juice over herself at the end of all of her vlogs. Color in all the juice bottles on this page.

JoJo is not afraid of getting **JUICED!**

JoJo's Juice

How many juice bottles can you count?

See answers on page 40

Sweet as a Heart

Keep drawing around and around this heart to create a cool pattern and fill this page. Then color it in and decorate with stickers.

Sassy Swatches!

I love designing new bows. Design some cool patterns for me to try on my next bow. Use the stickers to decorate these fabric swatches.

Hello, Cupcake!

Use the stickers and draw your own doodles to add faces and accessories to every cupcake on this page. It's time to create some super cute cupcake friends!

Use stickers to complete this poster.

Please ask an adult to help you cut this page out!

Bow Sequences

JoJo really loves bows! They are part of her signature style.

Figure out which bow completes each sequence going down, using the stickers!

Super-style Diary

Use the stickers to style JoJo for a week, then write a diary entry about what JoJo did each day and why her style was AWESOME!

Monday

Sticker

Write about JoJo's day: ....
....
....
....

Tuesday

Sticker

Write about JoJo's day: ....
....
....
....

Wednesday

Sticker

Write about JoJo's day: ....
....
....
....

Thursday

Sticker

Write about JoJo's day: ....
....
....
....
....

Friday

Sticker

Write about JoJo's day: ....
....
....
....
....

Saturday

Sticker

Write about JoJo's day: ....
....
....
....
....

Sunday

Sticker

Write about JoJo's day: ....
....
....
....
....

27

Word Power

1. SWEET IS MY SWAGGER

2. BOWS MAKE EVERYTHING BETTER

28

3.

PEACE OUT HATERZ

BESTIES NOT BULLIES

4.

5.

BOWS ARE MY SUPERPOWER

See answers on page 40

Badge Club

Use your stickers to create some awesome JoJo-inspired pin badges. Design one for each of your BFFs.

SUPER CUTE

For:

For:

HAPPY THOUGHTS

For:

For:

JoJo Siwa

For:

For:

Cute Cutout!

Cut out this JoJo-inspired door sign and decorate it using your art skills and stickers.

This room belongs to:

Sticker Sums

Did you know that JoJo's favorite subject is math? Work out these sweet sums using the key and the stickers. Write your answers in the boxes.

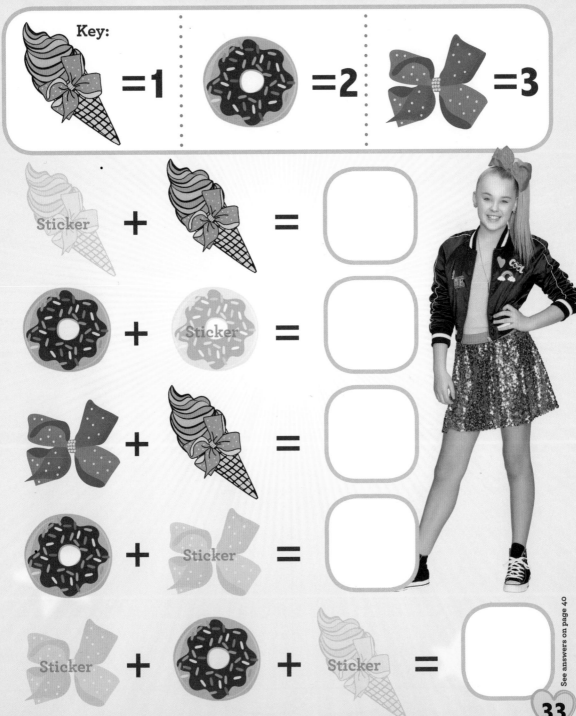

Key:

🍦 =1   🍩 =2   🎀 =3

Sticker + 🍦 = ☐

🍩 + Sticker = ☐

🎀 + 🍦 = ☐

🍩 + Sticker = ☐

Sticker + 🍩 + Sticker = ☐

See answers on page 40

Color Crazy!

It's time to channel your inner artist and make this page look super-special using your colors and stickers.

Word Search

Find the JoJo-inspired words in the puzzle below.
Look across, down, and diagonally.

G	H	I	Z	C	V	Y	B	A	T	O	P
E	L	T	U	F	R	N	K	O	S	M	E
S	A	S	S	Y	H	I	J	P	W	F	T
R	D	T	A	S	P	O	C	R	E	Y	M
N	I	A	D	W	J	O	X	Z	E	T	Q
P	E	R	D	J	U	Q	G	U	T	I	S
E	Z	D	T	Y	I	U	K	L	N	O	W
A	M	U	R	T	C	B	H	E	T	U	A
C	W	U	D	R	E	A	M	R	Y	P	G
E	X	S	A	P	L	Q	T	J	Z	U	G
W	A	C	H	I	E	V	E	H	D	B	E
Z	O	K	C	E	T	R	S	D	I	M	R

STAR **ACHIEVE**

JUICE **SASSY**

JOJO **SWEET**

BOW **SWAGGER**

DREAM **PEACE**

DREAM
BELIEVE
ACHIEVE

See answers on page 40

37

JoJo Shadows

Which shadows on the right match the pictures of JoJo on this page? When you know, place a number sticker next to the picture.

1.

2.

3.

4.

5.

Super Cute

CUTE & CONFIDENT

a.

b.

DREAM Crazy BIG

c.

SWEET

d.

e.

See answers on page 40

39

Answers

PAGE 9 Juicy Pairs

PAGES 10 AND 11
Bow-the-Difference

PAGES 14 AND 15 Puzzle Pics

a.

b.

c.

d.

PAGE 18 Juice Explosion!
There are 18 juices.

PAGE 25 Bow Sequences

PAGES 28 AND 29 Word Power
SWEET IS MY SWAGGER
BOWS MAKE EVERYTHING
   BETTER
PEACE OUT HATERZ
BESTIES NOT BULLIES
BOWS ARE MY SUPERPOWER

PAGE 33 Sticker Sums
ICE CREAM + ICE CREAM = 2
DOUGHNUT + DOUGHNUT = 4
BOW + ICE CREAM = 4
DOUGHNUT + BOW = 5
BOW + DOUGHNUT +
   ICE CREAM = 6

PAGE 37 Word Search

G	H	I	Z	C	V	Y	B	A	T	O	P
E	L	T	U	F	R	N	K	O	S	M	E
S	A	S	S	Y	H	I	J	P	W	F	T
R	D	T	A	S	P	O	C	R	E	Y	M
N	I	A	D	W	J	O	X	Z	E	T	Q
P	E	R	D	J	U	Q	G	U	T	I	S
E	Z	D	T	Y	I	U	K	L	N	O	W
A	M	U	R	T	C	B	H	E	T	U	A
C	W	U	D	R	E	A	M	R	Y	P	G
E	X	S	A	P	L	Q	T	J	Z	U	G
W	A	C	H	I	E	V	E	H	D	B	E
Z	O	K	C	E	T	R	S	D	I	M	R

PAGES 38 AND 39
JoJo Shadows
1) c
2) a
3) d
4) b
5) e

Stickers for decorating the activities!

Pages 2–3

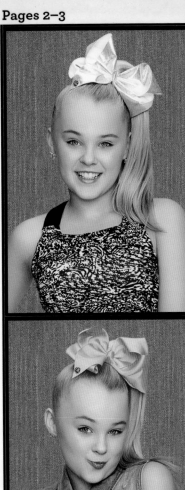

Page 4

Page 7

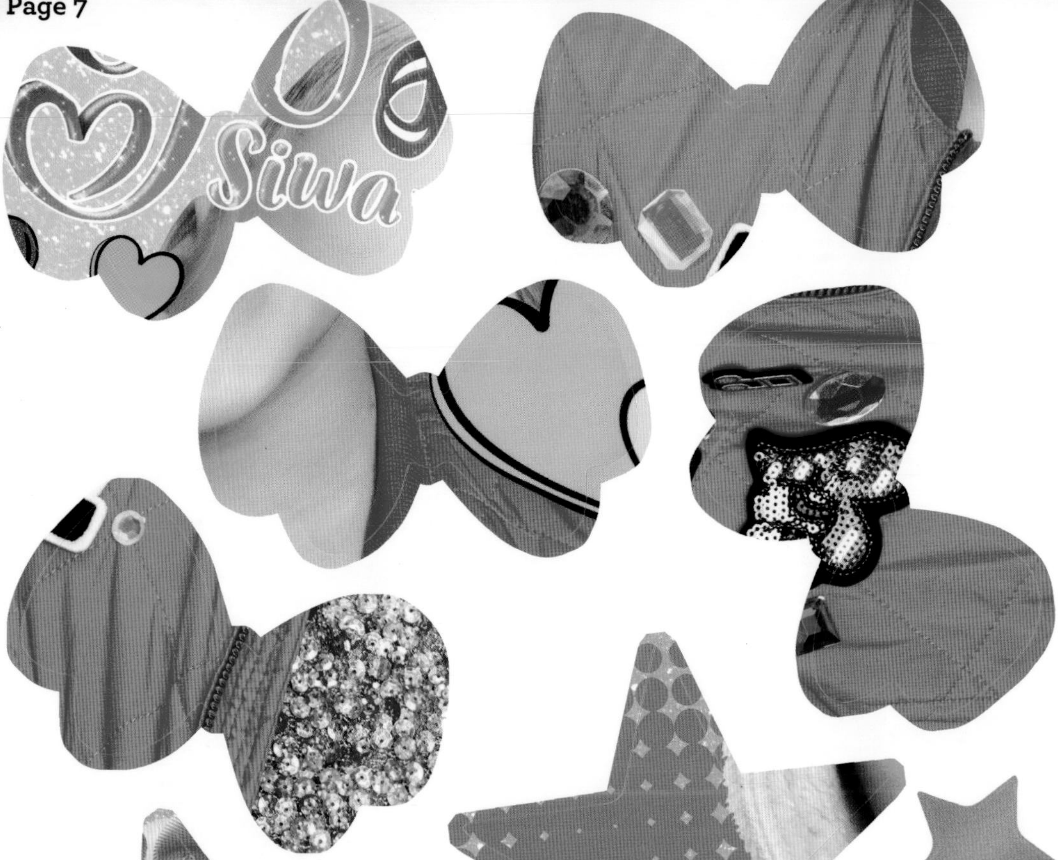

Page 8

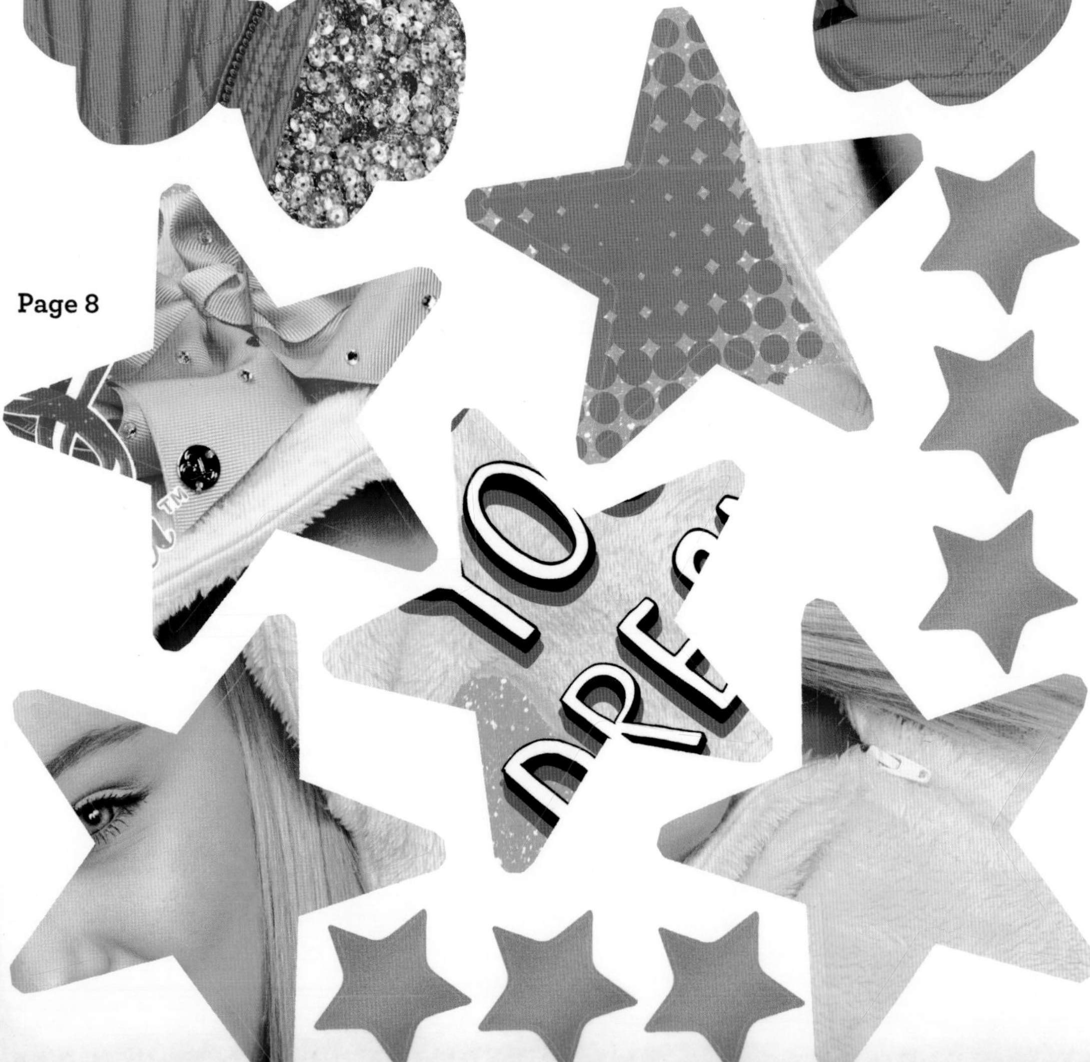

Pages 10—11

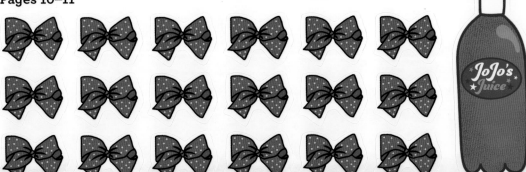

Pages 14–15

a.

b.

c.

Page 22

d.

Page 16-17

DREAM

SUPER

Star

Page 23

Page 24

Page 25

Pages 26–27

Pages 28–29

E S A G

W S ♥

KE RYT

SS

BE LL

PEOUHA

Page 30

DREAM Crazy BIG

BE You

Dream huge

BE You

SWEET IS MY SWAGGER

EAT DANCE SLEEP

Page 33

Page 35

Siwa™

Page 36

Page 39

1. 2.

3. 4.

5.

Stickers for decorating the activities!

DREAM **Crazy** BIG

BE **You**

Dream huge

BE **You**

SWEET IS MY **SWAGGER**

BOW Bow

BOWS MAKE EVERYTHING BETTER

From My Heart To Yours

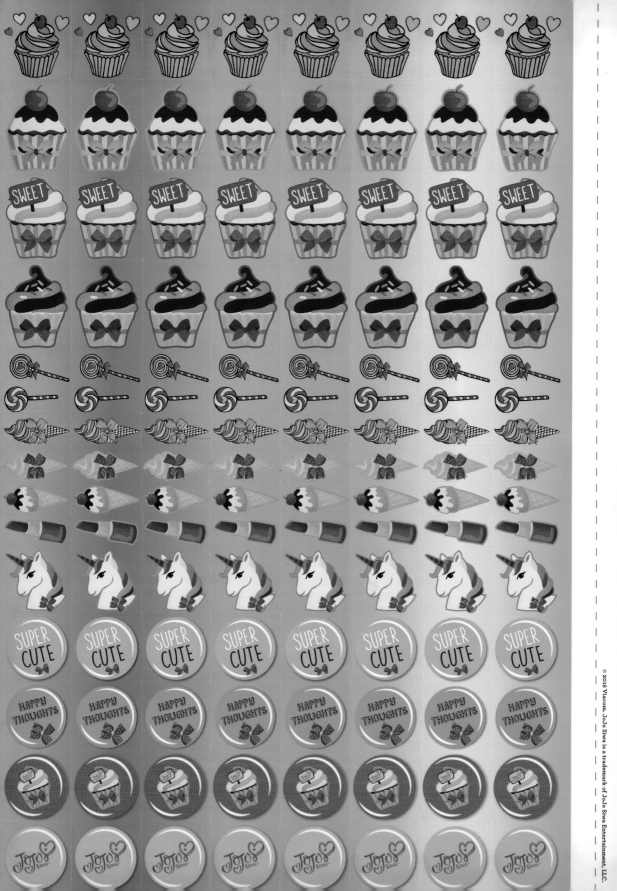

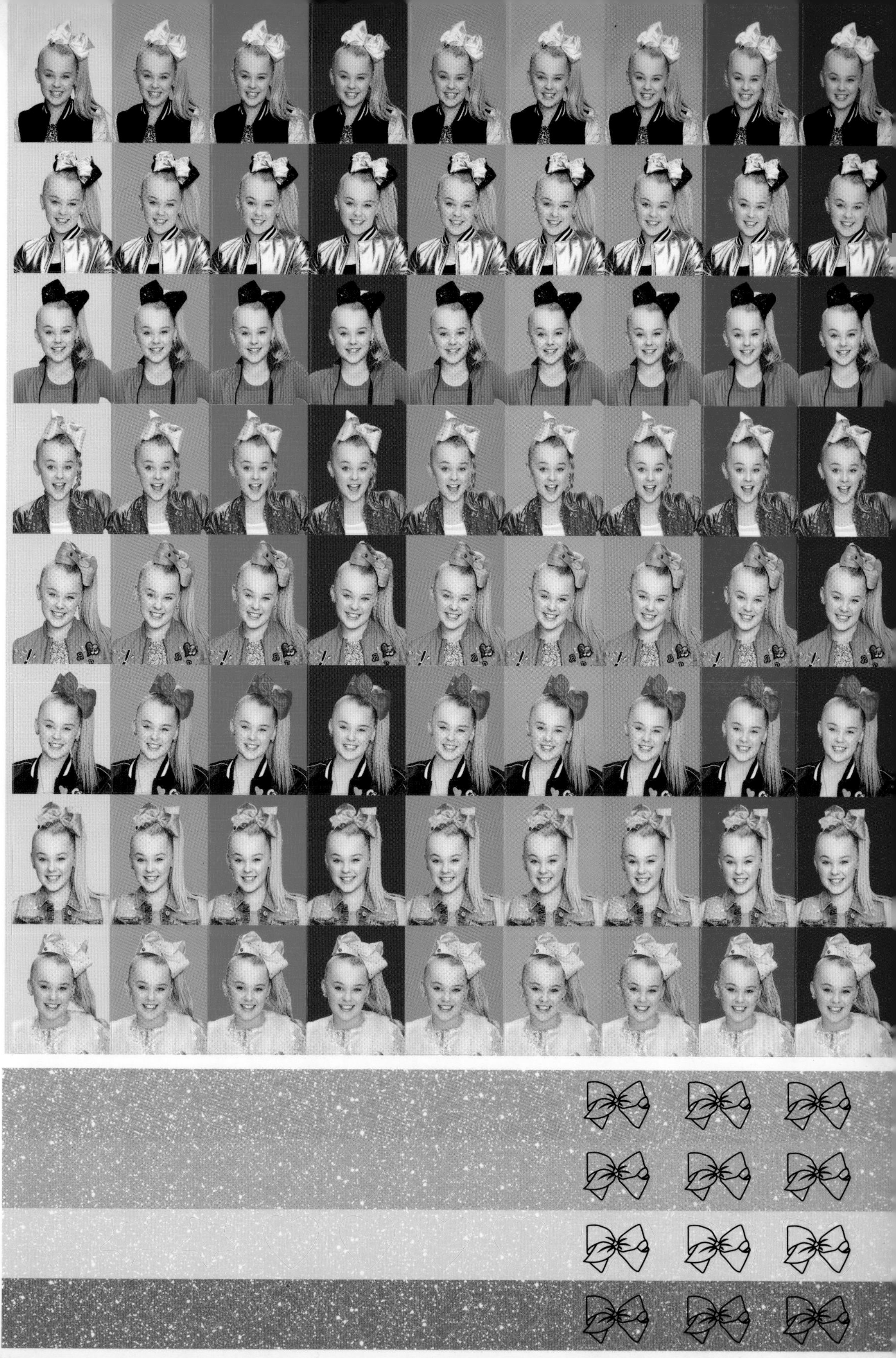